Guy Hunt
Governor Who Leveled The Field

Alice Yeager

Seacoast Publishing
Birmingham, Alabama

Guy Hunt: Governor Who Leveled The Field

Published by Seacoast Publishing, Inc.
1149 Mountain Oaks Drive
Birmingham, Alabama 35226

Library of Congress Control Number: 2010930602

Cover art by Thomas B. Moore

ISBN 1-59421-057-8

To obtain copies of this book, please write or call:
Seacoast Publishing, Inc.
Post Office Box 26492
Birmingham, Alabama 35260
(205) 979-2909

Alice Yeager

Contents

About The Series

Alabama Roots is a book series designed to provide reading pleasure for young people, to allow readers to better know the men and women who shaped the State of Alabama, and to fill a much-needed void of quality regional non-fiction for students in middle grades.

For years, teachers and librarians have searched for quality biographies about famous people from Alabama. This series is a response to that search. The series will cover a span of time from pre-statehood through the modern day.

The goal of Alabama Roots is to provide biographies that are historically accurate and as interesting as the characters whose lives they explore.

The Alabama Roots mark assures readers and educators of consistent quality in research, composition, and presentation.

It is a joint publishing project of Seacoast Publishing, Inc., and Will Publishing, Inc., both located in Birmingham, Alabama.

Alice Yeager

Foreword

Will Publishing, L.L.C., is proud to partner with Seacoast Publishing to sponsor this biography of Alabama Governor Guy Hunt. I am personally proud to have known Governor Hunt and his family and to have worked with him and his administration. This book will long serve as a reminder as to what good can come when people put service first. The men and women who gave up their normal lives in order to participate in Governor Hunt's tenure were dedicated public servants and I am honored to have served with them.

When Governor Hunt passed away in January 2009, an article about his death appeared in the *New York Times*. In reading that article, I saw both a challenge and an opportunity to help fulfill a special man's dream. In the article there was a direct quote from Governor Hunt that he made in 1998 when asked how he would like to be remembered. Hunt's answer was simply, "The thing that would thrill me the most is for every fourth-grade student in this state who reads Alabama history someday will have the understanding that this is an honest governor who ran an honest administration and would not knowingly violate the letter or the spirit of the law."

That was my purpose in seeing that his story was told.

It is important that future generations know his story and of the love he had for Alabama. Guy Hunt wasn't just a politician, he wasn't just a preacher; he wasn't just a farmer; he wasn't just a salesman. He was a man who worked hard, cared about Alabama and her people and who was willing to offer himself for service no matter the odds.

The Alabama Roots Biography Series is meant to help educate young people about great Alabamians and to hopefully inspire them to become great themselves. Overcoming obstacles and hard times; having a vision for the future; setting and accomplishing goals are but a few of the possibilities that come from inspired young people.

It is my hope that this book will help assure Governor Hunt's wish for future generations to really know him.

W. Edgar Welden
Will Publishing, L.L.C.

The Guy Hunt family in 1967. Guy, Helen and children, from left to right, Sherrie, 9; Keith, 7; Lynn, 4; and Pamela, 11.

Writing About Guy Hunt

I love Alabama, so writing about our state's rich history is something that I really enjoy. I've had the opportunity to write other books for the *Alabama Roots Series* and each time I begin by reading everything I can find about the person who will be the main character. Several books were used to gather information about former Governor Guy Hunt – *Alabama Governors (A Political History of the State)* by Webb and Armbrester was helpful, and I also read both of the inaugural souvenir booklets – *A New Day . . . A New Alabama* and *Alabama – The Best is Yet to Come*. A collection of writings by Guy Hunt himself, (*The Best of Elder Guy Hunt*), contained stories about important people in his life. Other information was found on the Internet and in newspaper articles shared by Hunt's friends and family members. I also watched several clips of interviews with Governor Hunt.

All of the sources mentioned above provided needed information, but the thing that was most help-ful was meeting members of the Hunt family and talking with life-long friends of Guy Hunt. I greatly appreciate Mrs. Edna Hicks, Mr. and Mrs. John Thomason, Mrs. Fay Mezzell, and Mr. Edgar Welden for taking time to share stories about their special friend. I quickly learned that Governor Hunt's friends are very protective of his memory – as good friends should be – and often when speaking of the former governor, they paused to choke back tears. They loved Guy Hunt dearly.

I also had the chance to meet Governor Hunt's widow, Anne Smith Hunt, and his son, Keith Hunt. They not only shared stories about the man who was a devoted husband and father, but they also shared photos that were used in this book. I appreciate their help and hope that I have been able to convey just how much Guy Hunt meant to so many people.

While writing this story, I learned a lot about our 54th governor that I had not previously known – he was the first Republican governor since the Recon-struction years that followed the Civil War; he was Alabama's first preaching governor; and he was the first governor with a special needs child who lived in the Governor's Mansion.

Guy Hunt: Governor Who Leveled The Field

I hope that you will enjoy reading about the man from Holly Pond who was elected not once, but twice, as our state's highest official.

Editor's Note: Sometimes the titles of books in the Alabama Roots Biography Series *are easy. This one wasn't. Every time we tried, it took too many words to explain why Governor Guy Hunt was so important. So we wanted to explain it a little bit.*

Some say Guy Hunt was an accidental governor...that the only reason he got elected was because Alabama voters were tired of the Democrats fighting among themselves. Whatever the reason, Guy Hunt did get elected and his election brought about one of the most important changes in Alabama politics and government in the past century.

Until his election, the Democrats held government and political power. When the Republican Hunt won, that all changed. Alabama became a place where both Democrats and Republicans had an equal chance of getting elected. Some people called it "leveled the field." Since Governor Hunt was a farmer, using the word "field" in the title seemed like a fun idea.

One thing is for sure, Guy Hunt plowed some new ground for his political party.

Alice Yeager

Governor Guy Hunt with President Ronald Reagan

Guy, a Holly Pond boy in overalls with his dog, on the steps of his farmhouse home.

Prologue

IF YOU TRAVEL TO HOLLY POND, Alabama, you will pass through roadside communities with not-so-usual names. Depending on which way you're heading, you will notice communities with pleasant names that make you want to stop and visit – names like *Pilgrim's Rest*, *Birdsong* and *Gum Pond*.

You will find a handful of businesses and, of course, as in any small Alabama town, you will find several churches. When the doors are opened, these churches are filled with people who believe the Lord meant what he said about the Sabbath . . . remember it and keep it holy.

Fewer than 700 people live in Holly Pond today and the family names found on mailboxes dotting the highway – Holcombe, Hopper, Holmes and Hunt – are the same names found on moss-covered markers in church graveyards. People born in Holly Pond tend to stay there, and if they move away, they tend to return when its time for burying.

Most families in this rural community farm the same land that their parents and grandparents poured sweat into. They have learned to make the best with whatever life offers, and when times are tough, they work hard and pray harder. Nobody has a lot, but they've learned to make do.

Everybody knows everybody else. If there is an illness, friends and neighbors show up to help out. If there is a death, the same friends and neighbors show up with casseroles and comforting words.

This is the life that Harold Guy Hunt, Alabama's 54th governor, was born into during the summer of 1933.

Just as his family before him, Guy Hunt grew up farming the land and preaching from the Good Book every chance he got. During his campaign for governor, the people running against him made sure that everyone knew these things – his opponents wanted others to know that Guy Hunt was a preaching farmer from a small town that few Alabamians had heard of. They were quick to poke fun at his country-boy roots.

But Alabama voters liked Guy's plain-spoken ways, his Sunday preacher lifestyle and his genuine love for his state, so they put Harold Guy Hunt in the governor's office. Soon after Governor Hunt took office, even his opponents began to realize that there are lessons to be learned when studying the Bible . . . while sweating over crops . . . and when knowing your neighbors well enough to know that they're hurting. His election was historic for many reasons, but he will always be remembered as the first Republican governor since Reconstruction – changing Alabama from a state ruled by Democrats to a state where both Democrat and Republicans stood a chance of getting elected.

Guy and son, Keith, together on the Hunt's tractor—farmers, just as their ancestors who settled Holly Pond.

Alice Yeager

Cullman County, Alabama

(A place filled up with good farmers . . .)

PEOPLE WHO LIVE IN CULLMAN COUNTY today still enjoy many of the things that appealed to the first people who lived there. Long before Alabama became a state, Cherokee Indians found living off the land to be an easy way of life. Along with rich soil for planting crops, they found streams filled with fish; thickets filled with geese, ducks, and wild turkeys; and woods filled with deer, rabbits, squirrels and other wildlife. Life was good, but during the 1830s the American government forced the Indians to leave their north Alabama homes.

Thirty years later, a German named Colonel John G. Cullmann decided to come to America, the land of opportunity as it was called, in search of a better life.

Colonel Cullmann arrived in 1866, just after the Civil War ended, and searched for the perfect place to start his dream colony. He found exactly what he was looking for and wrote to his family still in Germany, asking them to join him in America, "After traveling around the country and arriving in North Alabama the impression was made upon my mind that if this country was filled up with good farmers it would be the garden spot of America. I found here all that I had been looking for . . ."

A handful of German families loaded up their belongings, left their homes, and moved to Alabama. They formed a colony, and by 1873, the colony officially became a town. Its citizens honored the German colonel by naming the new town after him – slightly changing the spelling by dropping the last "n" from Cullmann's name. The town and its county became known as *Cullman*.

In only a few years others made their way to the area. Farmers in nearby Georgia heard rumors of fertile Alabama lands that could be bought at cheap prices, and they wanted to be a part of this thriving farming community, too. The Germans welcomed the Georgia farmers and the two groups worked well together while sharing crop-growing tips they found to be successful.

The farmers experimented to see which fruits and vegetables would grow best in Alabama's soil and climate. The Germans and the Georgians learned to grow different crops from year to year so that the soil would remain full of nutrients. Grapes and strawberries, along with vegetables such as corn and potatoes, grew well in Cullman County. Cotton crops soaked up the summer sun and burst into fluffy white balls which were harvested for good money.

The colony of farmers believed in hard work but they knew that having fun was important too. People gathered for picnics and band concerts, and they built churches that became an important part of their social lives. Cullman became known as a caring community where neighbors helped each other during hard times. If a family lost their home to fire or storms, others pitched in and rebuilt the house. If a neighbor fell ill and could not work, others tended his crops and nursed him back to health.

Colonel Cullmann died in 1895 at age 70, but today people in Cullman County will proudly tell you that this area continues to be *filled up with good farmers . . .* and that when it comes to successful farming practices, Cullman is still considered one of the leading counties in Alabama, and the nation. They are also quick to point out that small-town hospitality is alive and well – the people of Cullman County still pride themselves in taking care of their own.

This is the pond—as it appears today—for which Holly Pond was named.

Alice Yeager

More Georgia Farmers

TWO YEARS AFTER Cullman became a town, a newly-married Georgia couple in search of a good place to live passed through Cullman County. About 15 miles before reaching town, the young husband and wife stopped to take an overnight break. They set up camp near a large pond surrounded by holly bushes, and when daylight came the couple looked over the rolling pastures and woodlands thick with timber. They saw no need to go further. The man and wife unloaded belongings and decided to start their new life near the watering spot where they had rested. Soon others joined the couple and after considering several names, the pioneers decided to name the area after the very thing that first caught their eye—the shiny green-leafed holly bushes surrounding the pond. They called their community *Holly Pond*.

In 1912 another Georgia farmer found his way to

Holly Pond. His name was W.O. Hunt, but most people called him Otto. He was a farmer, a carpenter and a Primitive Baptist preacher.

Otto met and married a local girl named Orene Holcombe and after marrying, Otto moved back to Georgia with his new bride. They didn't stay long. A year later, the Hunts returned to Holly Pond and bought a forty-acre farm on the outskirts of town. The young husband worked hard, cleared his land, and built a simple but sturdy house so that he and Orene could start a family.

A baby daughter was born in 1913, and by 1925 four healthy boys had been added to the family. Having strong boys to help with chores was a blessing for farming families that worked from sunup to sundown. Otto paid off the farm and bought a car. Things were going well for the Hunt family until one fall day in 1927.

Alice Yeager

The Christian Thing to Do

AUTUMN IN ALABAMA means harvesting time. Families were so busy in the fields, schools closed for several weeks so children could stay home and help bring in the crops. Cotton was one of the many crops grown on the Hunt farm.

Alabama soil and warm temperatures made their land a good place to grow cotton. It wasn't easy; lots of sweat and hard work was needed before the cotton bolls could be picked. Planting began after the last spring frost, but it didn't take long for green stems to sprout, which meant that someone must work the fields with a hoe to make sure there was plenty of space between stalks and to chop down weeds that popped up around the cotton plants. By June, tiny white blossoms burst open and thrived during Alabama's sizzling summers. Farmers worked long, tiring hours underneath the blazing sun as they tended to the cotton plants, hoeing and hoping for rain to keep the summer heat from parching or drying up the cotton. By late August the blossoms began to shed, leaving a tiny boll or pod that opened. The boll contained fluffy, white cotton that was ready to be picked.

During cotton-picking season everybody in the Hunt family pitched in. Even the youngest children worked, usually twelve hours a day, stopping only an hour for lunch and to take a short rest or nap.

The prickly cotton plants tore at the pickers' hands. The razor-sharp prongs outside the boll protected the cotton, piercing fingers as they plucked the snowy-white plant from its grip. Cotton pickers hunched over and moved through row after row while weighted down by burlap bags strapped over aching shoulders. The bags grew heavier as the sun grew higher and the day grew longer. Most grown-ups could pick 400 pounds of cotton a day and it was not unusual for young children to pick as much as 25 to 50 pounds a day. Having a large family came in handy when working a farm.

After the cotton was picked, Otto hauled it to the Holly Pond cotton gin where the seeds were separated from the cotton. Removing the seeds was necessary for the cotton to be sold. During one trip to the gin, Otto was helping operate the machinery when something went wrong. He reached into the machine to see if he could figure out why the gin wasn't working and the machine grabbed his right hand. It chopped off one finger and held the others so fiercely that Otto couldn't free his hand.

With help, Otto finally loosened his hand, and a friend rushed him to the doctor. An operation was needed to stop the bleeding. With injuries like this, doctors usually amputated the whole hand to stop infection. Otto didn't want to have his hand cut off. He pleaded with a friend to stay in the operating room and stop the doctor from removing his injured hand. The friend did what Mr. Hunt asked, and the doctor left the hand attached. It took a long time to heal and Otto was in a lot of pain, but at least he still had his hand.

While he recovered, Otto's neighbors showed up to help. They joined the older boys and gathered crops. His right hand remained stiff for the rest of his life, and because he was missing a finger, he could no longer pick 400 pounds of cotton a day. He could now only pick 100 pounds with his good hand, but he never complained.

A few of Otto's friends questioned if perhaps the accident could have been avoided. They thought that if the equipment hadn't gotten stuck, maybe Otto would not have lost his hand. They wondered if the injured farmer would file a lawsuit or take the gin's owner to court and try to get money from him, but Mr. Hunt never placed the blame on anyone other than himself.

Besides, Otto felt that suing a person just wouldn't be the Christian thing to do.

Harold Guy Hunt

TIME PASSED AND OTTO LEARNED to move the fingers on his right hand enough to grip his work tools. He learned to rely on his left hand, and soon became quite good at using a saw and hammer again. People in Holly Pond considered him a fine carpenter.

Less than two years after Otto's accident, Orene gave birth to another son. The Hunt's named him Hubert. He lived less than a month. The family never knew why baby Hubert died – they just accepted it as God's will and with broken hearts they went back to working their farm.

On June 17, 1933 the final child was born in the Hunt family. He was named Harold Guy Hunt and immediately Guy received lots of attention. Like most country babies born during this time of the Great Depression, Guy was born at home on the farm. His oldest sister would soon be twenty years old and his youngest brother was almost eight years old. Since they had lost baby Hubert only four years earlier, the

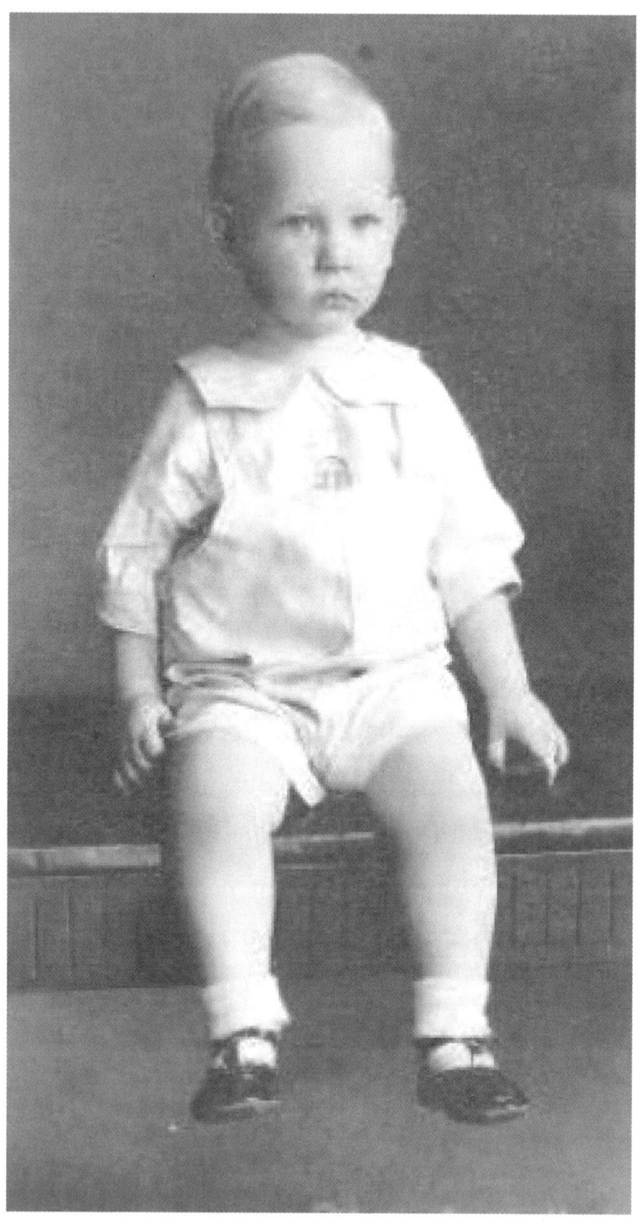

Guy as a baby.

whole family watched over little Guy and made sure that he was well taken care of.

During the Depression people were without jobs and banks ran out of money. Many people lost their homes and couldn't afford such necessities as food and warm clothing.

Many Alabamians survived with little or no money.

Only a few years before Guy's birth, a man named Benjamin Meek Miller was elected governor of Alabama. He won the election just as the Depression began. Once a governor is elected, there is usually a parade to celebrate his inauguration day – the day he takes office. Governor Miller's inauguration day wasn't that exciting . . . only two automobiles travelled the parade route because Miller was determined not to waste gasoline. He also brought one of his favorite cows to the governor's mansion so money wouldn't have to be spent on milk and butter. People said that Governor Miller also tried to save money while living at the mansion by using only one light bulb. Some say that he carried the bulb from room to room and screwed it into a socket when he needed light. Times were tough.

The Depression had been particularly hard on Alabama farmers because no one had money to buy their crops. This meant that many farmers couldn't keep up the payments on their land or pay for their farming supplies. When this happened, the banks took the farmers' homes and their farms. The Hunt family struggled, but Otto believed that if you had debts, you were supposed to pay them. He believed that a man's word was important and if you promised to pay someone, then you should keep your promise even if it meant working harder and doing without.

Growing up during the Depression and watching his papa left Guy with strong memories that he carried with him for the rest of his life. Even though he was born into poverty, Guy's family worked hard, grew their own food and managed to somehow keep their home. As a child Guy didn't realize they were poor because none of their neighbors or friends had any more than his family. To him, working hard and doing without was how everyone lived.

Being the baby of the family, Guy enjoyed getting attention from his older brothers and his sister, and he loved the way his mother watched out for him. Mrs. Hunt was tender hearted and teared-up easily when it came to her children. Everything they did became a special memory for her, and one of those memory-making moments came when Guy was a toddler. Guy was feeling all grown up because he was finally old enough to wear britches like his older brothers. He was also proud because he had learned to put them on all by himself. But one day after pulling the pants up, something began to sting his legs. Little Guy screamed and carried on so that his parents came running to see what was wrong. A yellow jacket had crawled inside Guy's corduroy pants and it hadn't liked sharing the pants with a squirming boy. As soon as Otto got the pants off of his son and saw what the problem was, a misty-eyed Mrs. Hunt said, "Bless his little heart, and he was putting on his own britches."

Not long after the yellow jacket accident, two-year-old Guy ran into more problems. One day he gathered a bunch of green apples and before anyone noticed, he had eaten a belly full. Right away his stomach began to hurt. The pain grew worse and eventually turned into an illness called *colitis* which sometimes caused people to die.

Little Guy couldn't eat without throwing up his food. He grew so weak that he couldn't walk and the family didn't think he was going to make it.

The doctor suggested that Mrs. Hunt try feeding the sick child a new food he had been hearing about. Luckily, it stayed in Guy's tummy. The new food was called Jell-O, and for little Guy Hunt it was a life saver.

Even though times were hard, farm life was fun

for Guy. He had a dog named Bobby that was part bulldog, and the two of them liked to explore the yard and nearby fields. They knew to stay in their own yard and not cross over into the neighbor's pasture where a black jersey bull pawed the ground and snorted when anyone came too close.

Bobby protected Guy. The dog's bark was different when trouble was around, so the grown-ups learned to listen. They could tell from Bobby's yelps when they needed to run out and check on their youngest son. The brave little dog was feisty and more than once he grabbed a copperhead snake in his teeth, shaking it to death before it could reach little Guy.

But the carefree days didn't last long for the youngest member of the Hunt family. By the time he was five years old, Guy's day began when he climbed out of bed at 5:30 in the morning to milk the cows. After that, he shucked corn, using the kernels of corn to feed the chickens, and saving the shucks to feed the cows. He kept the firewood box filled and hoed the weeds that poked up between the corn rows and cotton plants. His mother assigned him inside chores like sweeping and mopping floors, and washing and drying the dishes.

When he crawled into to bed at night, he was tired. It seemed that no sooner had he laid his head on the pillow, he would hear his Papa's voice calling, "time to get up."

Guy, front row on right, with parents and other family members. Standing, left to right, are Alvin, Grover, Lessie, Owen and Henry. Seated are Guy's father, Otto, and Mother, Orene.

Alice Yeager

Starting to School

WHEN GUY TURNED SIX, he started to school. He listened to his older brothers talk about Holly Pond School and he wasn't so sure he wanted to go. He worried, *what if he didn't know as much as the other children?* Seeing so many students at school scared him to death. There were big kids and little kids, and for a six-year-old like Guy who hadn't been away from home much, it seemed like there were *lots* of them. And another thing, all the school buses looked alike. How was he supposed to know which one would take him home at the end of the day?

But soon Guy realized he was good at being a student in school. Learning came easy to him and even though he was shy, he made friends easily. He loved his teachers and they certainly liked this small boy with polite manners who always remembered to say, "yes ma'am" and "no ma'am." Guy constantly thought of his mother's words – the same words that she said each and every time he and his brothers left the farm,

"Now, y'all remember to be good boys." His mother also reminded him to always be honest, "and no matter what you do, *always* tell the truth." Guy's make-my-mama-proud manners impressed his teachers.

Things were going pretty well until the second part of first grade.

Today children are vaccinated or given shots so they will not get sick with illnesses such as chicken pox, whooping cough, or the measles.

When Guy was young there were no shots to prevent those diseases. Everyone expected to catch them sooner or later, but not all of them at one time!

Guy's problem was that just as his chicken pox rash dried up, along came the measles, bringing on another skin rash *plus* a runny nose and fever. Guy had reddish-brown blotches all over his body.

On top of that, he caught the whooping cough before his chicken pox and measles had gone away. Guy's breathing passages become irritated and swollen, which led to terrible coughing spells. He coughed so much it was hard to breathe. Whooping cough gets its name from the sound that people make when they gasp for air. While coughing non-stop, sometimes Guy would take in a sudden gulp of air, and as the fresh air made its way through the swollen airways, it would make a "whooping" noise.

Guy lay in bed running a fever and coughing his head off for a month. Fever often comes with measles and whooping cough and sometimes the fever is so bad that it can cause brain damage or make people have crazy thoughts. Guy frightened his mama and papa when he woke up from time to time and told them that he was dead. His family gathered around and tried to convince him that he was alive . . . very ill . . . but alive.

Just like the time Guy had been so sick from eating too many green apples, Mr. and Mrs. Hunt worried that their little boy might die. After several weeks, Guy's fever broke, and he started getting better. However, when he went back to school he was all skin and bones. His classmates took one look at the dark circles under their friend's dull, blue eyes and they noticed his frail body. He looked so sickly, they all wondered if he still might possibly die.

When he returned to school, Guy had trouble paying attention. Learning was harder for him than it had been before he got sick. His teacher, Mrs. Bessie Carnell, knew how ill he had been and she was very patient. She was so kind and understanding, Guy thought of her as an angel.

Guy tried to join in at recess but his body was still weak and he had little energy. He wasn't completely over his cough and if he played hard, the coughing got worse. When that happened, he just stood to the side and watched while his friends ran and played. As time passed, learning became easy again, but it took much longer for his thin body to grow stronger.

Alice Yeager

Double Promotion

BY THE END OF THE SECOND GRADE every-
thing seemed back to normal, even better than normal.
Guy found himself with two sweethearts at the same
time – one was Betty at school and the other was
Imogene at church. This didn't work out very well,
however. It wasn't long before the school sweetheart
learned about Guy's church sweetheart and both girls
soon found new boyfriends. Other than losing two
girlfriends, the year was a great success. His teacher,
Miss Louise Mullins, made learning fun and always
encouraged her students to do their best.

When the next school year rolled around, Guy
was expecting to enter the third grade but one of his
brothers happened to look at the back of Guy's report
card. Miss Mullins hadn't said anything about it to Guy,
but she had written a note saying that she was promot-
ing him from the second grade to the *fourth* grade. He
had done so well in her class, Miss Mullins thought
that Guy wouldn't need to sit through the third grade.

Skipping the third grade was an honor, but Guy soon learned that there were disadvantages. It took him a while to catch up with the older kids, plus he ran into a few bullies who were jealous of his double promotion. For the next few years, the bullies picked on Guy and called him names. They also made fun of his papa's name – calling him "squatto" instead of Otto . . . "Well lookie here, if it isn't the little *sissy boy* . . . aren't you *Squatto* Hunt's boy?" Guy knew that his papa didn't approve of fighting, which was just as well. The boys were much bigger than Guy and prob- ably would have beaten him black and blue. He also knew that if he got into trouble at school, he would be in big trouble when he got home.

Alice Yeager

Busier Than Ever

LUCKILY, AS THE STUDENTS GREW OLDER, Guy ended up being friends with some of the very bullies that had teased him. He joined them at recess to play baseball or to shoot marbles. Sometimes they even tossed jackknives in a game of mumbly-peg. By the time Guy reached middle school, he was getting over his shyness and realized that he had a talent for talking and giving speeches.

Even as a young boy, people noticed that Guy was a deep thinker, and he won all of the speaking contests that he entered. After listening to Guy speak, other students stopped bothering to enter contests because they knew that Guy would always win. But his classmates were okay with that, in fact, the students stood and cheered each time their friend finished his speeches.

While school was going well, times were tougher at home. Several of Guy's brothers left home to fight in World War II. Guy was eight years old when Japanese soldiers bombed Pearl Harbor in 1941. When the older Hunt boys joined the army, only Guy and his brother Grover were left to help on the farm. They worked harder to make up for the ones who had gone off to war. Guy watched his mama grow older with worry – which made him try even harder to make her proud of him – hoping that this would help take her mind away from her boys who were far away from Holly Pond fighting for their country.

His papa, Otto, was often called away to preach, leaving Guy with even more responsibilities at home.

In junior high, the hard-working boy milked three cows before leaving for school each morning. After school, he milked the cows again, and then it was time to feed the mules, the chickens and the hogs before heading to the fields. Guy plowed and hoed until it was too dark to see, and even though he was ex-hausted, he always took time to do his homework. He studied by the light of a coal oil lamp, sometimes late into the night. Each time Guy thought of giving up, he remembered what was expected of him. His Mama had raised him to work without complaining and to always do his best. Since his sister and brothers had all gradu-ated at the top of their classes, this was expected of Guy, too. Even with all of his chores, Guy continued to be on Holly Pond's A honor roll.

A teenage Guy Hunt.

Not only did Guy keep up his grades, but some-how he even found time to do extra activities at school. He entered school plays because memorizing the lines came easy for him, and he was a good actor. He played basketball for the Holly Pond High Broncos. Being tall and lanky helped in basketball, and he also had a good shooting arm. Classmates elected Guy president of the Future Farmers of America, and he also wrote stories for the school newspaper.

People noticed that Guy Hunt could do anything that he set his mind to do. One of his teachers, Mr. Carnell, surprised him by telling the class that Guy would probably be a U.S. Senator one day. The thought that something so special could happen to him had never crossed Guy's mind. Could a farmer's son from Holly Pond dare to dream such a thing?

Alice Yeager

Life After Holly Pond High

BY THE 10th GRADE, Guy decided to take as many classes as possible and graduate early. He completed all of the classes needed to finish school in two years and, at age 16, Guy graduated as class salutatorian. This meant that out of the 43 seniors in his class, he had the second highest grade average. All of his brothers and his sister had been valedictorians which meant that they graduated at the very top of their class, but since Guy was almost two years younger than most of his classmates, being salutatorian was certainly an honor.

The principal knew that Guy was smart enough to go to college. Guy liked the idea and wanted to take college classes to become a radio broadcaster. Talking had always been easy for him; in fact, his school yearbook listed things that seniors might leave to their younger classmates in a section called the "Last Will and Testament." For Guy, someone had written, "To anyone with the ability, we leave Guy's art of speaking."

The Hunts had no money to send Guy to college, but the principal didn't let that stop him. He wrote a letter to the University of Alabama and told them what a hard-working student Guy would be, and the university offered him a scholarship. But the more Guy thought about it, he knew that he was needed on the farm. He was the last child left at home, and since his parents were getting older, it wasn't as easy for them to work nonstop and to keep up with a forty-acre farm. Also, many of the boys in his class had gone away to fight in the Korean War and Guy knew that it wouldn't be long until the Army needed him too.

Alice Yeager

Mount Vernon Primitive Baptist Church

AS A TEENAGER, Guy began to wonder, *Should he become a preacher?*

It was a natural question. His papa preached. Both of his grandfathers preached, and so did one great grandfather. Several of his uncles had also been elders or speakers in the Primitive Baptist Church.

Guy grew up going to church each time people gathered because his parents believed that there were no excuses for not being in church. He liked the simple worship services and the friendly, but small, congregation at Mt.Vernon. People started arriving about 10:30 on Sunday mornings with all age groups joining together for singing. Musical instruments weren't used because the Primitive Baptists believed that the human voice was the only instrument needed in church. Some members even took special lessons to learn four-part harmony singing, and Guy thought the sound of blended voices coming out of the little church was beautiful. His mama's voice was so sweet and full of love, each time she sang, chills ran up Guy's spine. He loved to listen to her and he had a pretty good voice himself. Sometimes he was called on to lead the singing. Guy even came up with a different version of his favorite song, *Amazing Grace*. He sang its words to a peppier tune, and people called it *Amazing Grace* – Guy Hunt style.

After about thirty minutes of music, there was plenty of time for praying before the sermons began. When the actual preaching started, children stayed

Guy, left, breaking bread with friends.

with the grown-ups because the congregation thought that all ages should worship together. The elders or men who felt the call to preach would take turns speaking. Sometimes their messages were short, sometimes stomachs started growling before the elders finished preaching, but the ladies in the church had a remedy for that. This was another reason Guy loved his church – the ladies at Mount Vernon Primitive Baptist Church sure knew how to cook!

Often the church members gathered for lunch after the sermons ended and every family would bring a "potluck" dinner. This meant that everybody cooked their favorite foods and brought them to share with others. When all the foods were spread out on tables, Guy piled his plate high with homegrown vegetables like black-eyed peas, butter beans, corn, tomatoes, squash, okra, and more. He always found room for desserts, and his mama's peach cobbler was his favorite.

Helen Hunt as a young woman.

Helen

STILL IN HIS TEENS, Guy found yet another reason that he liked church. The reason had a name . . . Miss Helen Chambers.

Guy had not thought a lot about girls, at least not since the second grade when he had been dumped by two girls at one time. But now that he had finished school, he noticed some of the pretty young faces at church, especially the one belonging to Helen Chambers.

Helen was a year younger than Guy and since they grew up together in church, he always thought of her as just another childhood friend. But now that Helen was about to turn 16, Guy noticed her in a whole new way. He no longer saw a little girl with short hair and glasses. Now he saw a beautiful teenager with sparkling eyes and silky, soft brown hair. The love bug had taken a bite out of Guy Hunt and he could hardly take his eyes off of Helen. But when Guy showed up at Helen's 16th birthday party, Helen didn't pay much attention to him.

Helen's parents were farmers and she knew all about the back-breaking work needed to grow crops. She had decided she would *not* marry a farmer. And besides, she had a crush on another boy and kept watching for him to show up on her birthday. Guy was not about to give up, even if he did end up sitting with Helen's parents for most of the party, drinking lemonade and trying to find the courage to ask their daughter for a date.

Later that summer Guy did find the courage and luckily, Homer Chambers gave permission for his daughter to go out with the young man who had sipped lemonade with him during Helen's birthday party.

Guy and Helen double-dated with another couple and the night was perfect. The four teenagers drove to a drive-in movie near Cullman, and even though Guy didn't think it was possible, Helen looked even more beautiful in the glow of a late summer's moon. After their date, he couldn't think of anything but Helen and two short weeks later he told her just how he felt. Just before the Sunday morning church service, he took one look at the 16-year-old beauty and his already racing heart began to beat even faster. Her blue outfit made her eyes seem even bluer and somehow he found the courage to say, "I love your dress . . . and I love the one wearing it." Helen's heart melted and the teenagers knew that they wanted to spend the rest of their lives together.

The two couldn't stand to be apart, but there was little money to spend on dating. Guy wished he could take Helen to Cullman and treat her to his favorite meal at the Busy Bee Café – a hamburger and a coke – both for the grand total of ten cents. But dimes were hard to come by, so instead of going into town, they stayed at Helen's house.

It was not the ideal location for a date. The Chambers house was small and Helen had three younger brothers and a little sister. The young sweethearts sat in the kitchen to be alone, but it seemed that every time they started talking, Helen's brothers came running in the kitchen to get a drink of water, and those boys could put away a lot of water. Plus, Mr. Chambers wasn't sure he wanted his 16-year-old daughter getting serious with a boy, any boy. Bedtime at Helen's house came early, and if Guy had not left by 9 o'clock, Mr. Chambers dropped his shoe on the floor letting everyone know it was time for the date to end.

Guy decided there was only way to get Helen all to himself. It was fall of 1950, and after selling his first bale of cotton for $200, the lovesick teenager drove to

Cullman and spent his entire earnings on a wedding ring.

Alice Yeager

Springtime, Buttercups and Wedding Bells

JUST SEVEN MONTHS after her 16th birthday, Helen Chambers gladly put aside her promise not to marry a farmer and became Mrs. Guy Hunt. It had taken only a few dates for Helen to realize that Guy was much more than a farmer; he was a gentleman who always treated her with respect.

Still, it hadn't been easy convincing Helen's or Guy's family to let them get married at such young ages, no matter how much they told everyone they were in love. But soon both families consented. The sweethearts chose Sunday morning, February 25, 1951 as the wedding date and the marriage took place at Helen's home. Otto Hunt asked Helen and Guy to repeat their wedding vows in front of a small gathering of family and friends.

Guy Hunt: Governor Who Leveled The Field

Spring was in the air, buttercups were blooming, and Guy had never seen anything more beautiful than the 100-pound, five-foot-one, 16-year-old that answered "I do" when asked if she would "take this man to be her husband."

The newlyweds lived with Guy's parents until fall when they finally moved into a small building on the Hunt's farm. It wasn't much – there were cracks in the floors and walls, rain pelted the tin roof, and there was no running water which meant no indoor bathroom – but to Guy and Helen, the tiny house was perfect.

The Prettiest Farmer, Army Life and Little Pamela

HELEN DECIDED that since she had married a farmer, she might as well make the best of it and she wanted to help. She fed the chickens and gathered eggs, she picked cotton and helped with the crops, and she even worked beside her husband in the fields. Guy thought that his bride was the prettiest farmer he had ever seen.

Along with farming, Guy decided to buy 400 egg-laying hens and sell their eggs for extra money. Guy and Helen drove the eggs to Birmingham and sold them door-to-door. The egg business was tiring, but it brought in much needed money. The hours were long and Guy sometimes had trouble staying awake during the drive back to Holly Pond, so Helen learned to drive and helped Guy with the egg route.

For three and a half years the newly-weds worked the farm and enjoyed the changing seasons. Summer brought plenty of fresh vegetables and fruits for Helen to can and preserve for winter months when icy cold winds found their way through the cracks of the honeymoon cottage which didn't bother the Hunt's . . . they were together and that's all that mattered. But half way around the world a war was raging. This war – the Korean War – would soon take Guy away from the life he loved.

World War II had ended when Guy was a young teenager and soon afterwards a little Asian nation called Korea divided itself into two parts – north and south. The South Koreans believed in life much like the life of people in the United States where freedom is valued. But like China and Russia, the North Koreans supported communism or the belief that government should control the people. When North Korea attacked South Korea during the summer of 1950, the United States sent troops to help keep the North Koreans from taking over.

Many of the young men Guy's age were already fighting in the Korean War. In July 1954, Guy volunteered to serve. It would have been easier to stay

Guy as a soldier during the Korean War era.

home with Helen, especially since she was expecting their first child, but the young husband remembered the sacrifices that his older brothers had made for their country during World War II. He remembered his family anxiously waiting for his brothers to return home. He remembered spending hours playing with piles of dirt in the fields, pretending that dirt clods were Germany, Italy and Japan, while rocks were America – his rocks always smashed the clods. Guy knew how much America meant to his family and he

Guy, Helen and Pam on Pam's first birthday.

knew it was now his turn to fight.

Guy waved goodbye to Helen from a Greyhound bus and headed off for eight weeks of basic military training in South Carolina. Growing up on a farm paid off. Guy was used to working under the scorching sun from sunrise to sunset. Other than missing his family, he made it through training better than most other recruits.

When it was time for the baby's birth, the Army gave Guy a two-week leave. He hitched a ride back to Holly Pond and made it back before the baby was born. In fact, when his two weeks were up, the baby still hadn't arrived, and the Army gave Guy permission to stay another three days.

When their daughter finally came, there were medical problems – Baby Pamela Hunt was born mentally retarded. Some people blamed the doctor and suggested that the Hunts sue him for money, but Guy and Helen didn't complain. They decided that God knew they would be just the right parents for their special daughter and they felt blessed to have her. And, just like his papa had felt after losing his finger, Guy didn't think that suing would be the right thing to do.

It was hard to leave Helen and his new baby daughter, but Guy soon headed back to complete his training. Later when he was assigned to Fort Riley, Kansas, he found a small apartment so Helen and Pamela could come to Kansas so they could all live together. It was far from home, and they had almost no money, but they were together. Guy Hunt felt like the luckiest man in the world.

A Growing Family

WITH THE KOREAN WAR WINDING DOWN, Guy wasn't needed overseas. After staying in Kansas for almost two years with the 101st Airborne Division, the Army finally told him that he could return home to Holly Pond.

While Guy was in the army, one of the men at their church helped out by running Guy's egg route, so luckily the Hunts were able to pick back up where they had left off. Once again Guy thought of college but they now had about 1,500 laying hens. The egg business, along with farming, kept the young couple busy. Guy continued to be active in church, and more and more churches were inviting him to speak at their services. In 1958 he was ordained a Primitive Baptist gospel minister and the Hunt family continued to grow. So once again, it was decided that college would have to wait.

Guy, Helen and their growing family. From left, Pamela, Sherrie and Keith.

The young family, now with three children, was outgrowing the honeymoon cottage. When Pamela was two, Sherrie came along in December 1956. Then a brother, Keith, was born in May 1959. Guy's papa offered to help his son build a house and the Hunt's dream house was built within shouting distance of their first cottage. The new house wasn't fancy – just a one-level, three bedroom house, but it did have an indoor bathroom with running water. Guy and Helen loved it. They loved the way trees surrounded it to provide privacy and to give the children plenty of room to play, yet they could easily wave to neighbors passing by on the small country road that ran in front of their home.

Helen filled the new house with homemade quilts and embroidered pieces she made with her own hands. She packed her cabinets with canned fruits and vegetables, yet still found time to help her husband around the farm.

Guy couldn't imagine life being better. He still worked all day and into the dark, but when he found a few minutes to relax, he watched baby calves scamper in the pasture, or he and Helen strolled through the woods. Their favorite season was spring when every-thing came back to life after bitter cold winters. Side-by-side they walked shaded pathways, breathing in sweet-smelling honeysuckle and marveling at the blossoming trees. Guy felt closer to God when he was outdoors and he and Helen could have been perfectly happy on their small farm for the rest of their lives.

Guy aboard Air Force One with President George H.W. Bush. Little did he know that his call to government service would lead to moments such as this.

Alice Yeager

Called to Serve

IN THE UNITED STATES there are two major political parties – Democrats and Republicans. But for as long as Guy Hunt could remember, there was only one party that mattered to Alabama voters – most people in Alabama claimed to be Democrats. This was a lesson Guy had learned when he was only in the sixth grade.

The 1944 presidential campaign was underway and Guy's teacher, Miss Suzie, decided that her class would hold their own election to see whether the students thought Franklin D. Roosevelt (a Democrat) should be re-elected, or if Thomas E. Dewey (a Republican) should become the new president. Of 30 sixth grade students, only three voted for Dewey. Guy was one of those three.

It didn't bother Guy to be different. His papa taught him to be independent and to think for himself. Otto Hunt (a Republican himself) grew up as a Georgia Democrat, but now he liked the Republican way of thinking better. He was quick to say that he didn't leave the Democratic Party. He said the party left him, which meant that he didn't agree with the party's new ideas.

Guy listened to his papa and to politicians as they talked about why they should be elected. Even as a seven-year-old he enjoyed sitting in front of the radio and listening to the presidential candidates and their campaign speeches. He liked it when Republican candidates talked about their vision for the future and about a better life for Americans.

The speeches excited Guy so much that he began to read everything he could find about the men who were hoping to be president. He constantly checked out books about famous people and one of his favorite Americans was Theodore Roosevelt, a Republican who became America's youngest president 30 years before Guy was born.

Now that he was grown, Guy still favored the Republican way of thinking. At the national level, sometimes his candidate won. But at the state level, Democrats were always the winners on Election Day.

The more he thought about government, the more he believed that Alabama needed more than one strong political party. He thought that Republicans should have as much a chance to get elected as Democrats. By his 27th birthday, Guy decided that he should put his beliefs to work. He organized Republicans in his own county and held meetings to ask people to run for office on the Republican ticket. He talked of needing good, honest people to run so that Alabama voters would have more than just one choice or one party to vote for on Election Day.

It was not easy. No one wanted to be a Republican in a state where there were two to three times more people voting as Democrats. They thought that being a Republican was a waste of time and energy.

Guy didn't give up. He kept right on asking good men to run for office. He didn't get anyone to answer *yes*, instead they challenged him . . . "If you believe

Guy, here with broccoli that he grew, was always happy on the farm. Public service called him away, but he returned as often as he could, to this life that gave him such satisfaction and pleasure.

what you're saying, why don't you run for office your-self?" Guy didn't have an excuse.

He and Helen were perfectly happy with their lives – living on the farm and watching their children grow. Guy knew that he had been called to preach and he enjoyed speaking to Primitive Baptists congregations. The more he heard the question "why don't *you* run for office," the more he wondered if he should run for office. Just as he had been called to preach – perhaps he was also being called to serve as a political candidate.

Alice Yeager

You Win Some, You Lose Some

GROWING UP, Guy had never thought about running for an elected office. He had never considered himself a politician. The day his teacher, Mr. Carnell, told the class that Guy would one day be a United States senator, Guy shrugged off the teacher's comments as a compliment – not something that would actually happen. But perhaps Guy's running for public office was simply meant to be . . . maybe it was in his blood. After all, his family members could trace their roots back to one of the most famous men who ever lived in the White House – President Abraham Lincoln.

Guy soon realized that he shouldn't ask others to do something that he was not willing to do himself. So in 1962, he signed up to run for his first public office. He ran for a chance to serve in the Alabama Legislature, but he lost to the Democratic candidate in the general election by about 1,000 votes. Guy was disappointed but he was determined not to give up. He would try again. Plus, with the birth of daughter Lynn in February 1963, it was a busy and happy time at home.

Two years later, in 1964, Lyndon Johnson was president of the United States. He was a Democrat. He had been vice president when President John Kennedy was killed in 1963. When President Kennedy died, Johnson took over as president.

1964 was the year that Americans elected a new president and Johnson was seeking to be elected president. It would be a tough campaign. A Republican U.S. senator from Arizona named Barry Goldwater was running against Johnson, and many Americans supported him. Goldwater was what people called a "conservative." It meant that he believed in things like a strong military, personal privacy, less government involvement in people's lives and a smaller and less expensive government.

Republicans all over the United States believed that if enough American voters believed the things that Goldwater believed, and if those voters would cast their ballots for a Republican presidential candidate, rather than a Democrat, then perhaps Republican candidates might win other elections, too.

Guy Hunt happened to be one of those Republican candidates running for office in 1964. This time he was trying to win the job of probate judge in Cullman County.

Barry Goldwater didn't get enough votes to beat Lyndon Johnson, but in some parts of America, especially in the South, many people switched to the Republican ticket on voting day. Alabama was one of those places, including Cullman County.

When the votes were counted, 31-year-old Guy Hunt became the youngest probate judge in Alabama and the first Republican to be elected to any office in Cullman County in 30 years.

Guy enjoyed being probate judge. He served people in many ways. He helped people who wanted to legally change their name. He helped families to divide the property of a loved one who died. He prepared wedding licenses and he married couples. He also helped with legal papers during adoptions.

Many elected officials worked their jobs and then went home to rest or relax, but as probate judge, Guy kept right on working on his farm. He even started cutting pulpwood to make extra money. Pulpwood is the wood used to make paper, and there were lots of trees on the Hunt farm that were perfect for pulpwood.

After feeding farm animals and working the fields, Guy cut down trees until midnight. The next morning he woke up early, climbed into his old timber truck, and unloaded the wood on his way to the courthouse. Some days he carried his business suit with him, and after reaching his office, he went to the bathroom and changed before starting his day as probate judge. Some days he left the house wearing his suit – people who passed him on the road thought this was a funny sight to see – a pulpwood truck loaded with wood but driven by someone wearing a suit and tie.

All this work was exhausting, but Guy had never known any other way to live. He knew how hard his parents had always worked. If bills needed to be paid, he found the strength to work a little harder. By 1969 there were four children in the Hunt family. Pamela now had a brother named Keith and two sisters, Sherrie and Lynn. In addition to their other jobs, Guy and Helen started selling Amway's lotions, vitamins and products for housecleaning to help with the cost of raising a growing family.

Someone once asked him how you could tell if an elected official was honest. He quickly answered, "If you find someone in office for a time and *still* in debt, he is usually an honest politician."

Guy was probate judge for six years and then was re-elected to the same office again in 1970. While serving in this office, he and Helen were invited to the governor's mansion in Montgomery. Walking through the mansion's sunroom, Helen looked at a friend and said, "You know, I think that Guy might want to run for Governor one day."

In only a few short years, Helen's prediction would come true.

While serving as Probate Judge, Guy had already fulfilled dreams far beyond the farm boy's wild imaginations. He had even made quite a name for himself among fellow Republicans at the national level, and in 1976 he was elected as chairman of the Alabama delegation to the Republican National Convention in Kansas City. As a youngster listening to the national conventions, he always scooted his chair closer to the radio just as the Alabama delegate called out the name of the person that this state wanted to represent Republicans in the Presidential election. Now *he* would be the voice that people from all over the United States would hear . . . *he* would be the person who spoke up to call the name of the person who Alabamians Republicans supported for President.

Just when Guy thought that he had surpassed all

possible political dreams, he was given the opportunity to run for Alabama's highest office of all – Governor of Alabama.

In 1978 Republicans chose Guy as their candidate for governor. That meant he would run for office against Democratic candidate Fob James. Like always, the Republican candidate was defeated. Guy received only one out of every five votes that were cast in the election.

Guy was discouraged, but the thought of giving up never crossed his mind. When it came to politics, Guy knew that sometimes you're the winner, and sometimes you're the loser. When friends and supporters gathered around to comfort him after losing the election he was the first to say, "Just because you lose some is no sign to quit."

Alice Yeager

Being in The Right Place At the Right Time

FOB JAMES MIGHT HAVE KNOCKED Guy Hunt down, but he didn't knock him out. When it was time for Alabama to choose a new governor in 1986, Guy was ready to try again.

First he had to convince Republicans that he should be the choice for their party. Two other Republican candidates wanted the chance to be governor too, but more votes were cast for Guy during the summer election, earning him the right to represent his party on November's Election Day.

At that same time, something lucky happened for Guy and the Republicans.

The Democrats were trying to choose their candidate for governor at the same time that Guy was winning the chance to be the Republican's choice. Lucky

Guy campaigning on the back of a flatbed trailer.

for the Republicans, the Democrats were arguing about election rules and whether one of their candidates had broken those rules. The newspapers carried stories about the bickering Democrats. Many voters did not approve of how the Democrats were behaving.

While the squabbling Democrats flooded the news, Guy spent day after day driving his old Plymouth all over the state asking Alabamians to vote for him. His crowds were small, but he was encouraged when shaking hands with people who told him they wanted a change in politics, and they wanted a choice on Election Day.

To Guy, it seemed as if the Democrats always had more money to spend, always drew bigger crowds when they gave speeches, and always had more television and newspaper reporters swarming around them. But since Democrats had been elected governor for many years, Alabama simply was not used to taking Republicans seriously.

Then came a big shift, and it came because the Democrats could not stop fussing among themselves. The top two Democratic candidates from the summer election were both powerful and well-known men, Lieutenant Governor Bill Baxley and Attorney General Charles Graddick. When a run-off was held to see which of these men would face Guy in the fall, Graddick received more votes. But some Democrats complained that Graddick broke their party's rules by luring Republicans to vote for him in the Democratic run-off, when only people who had voted in the Democratic primary were supposed to have cast their votes during the run-off election.

Democratic Party leaders discussed the problem and decided that because Graddick had ignored their rules, he should not be their candidate for governor. They replaced him with Bill Baxley.

The Democrat voters were mad. They didn't like seeing a committee replace the man they had chosen as their candidate with someone else.

As Guy drove around the state asking people to vote for him, he realized things were changing, and fast. People who had voted for Democrats all their lives were now coming up to Guy and telling him that this time they were going to vote for a Republican.

Guy's crowds grew larger. He began getting more donations and lots of attention. Some of the attention he was getting was good.

But as in most elections, his opponents made sure that there was some negative attention too.

The Democrats ran ads pointing out that Guy was a preaching chicken farmer and a small town boy who had never gone to college. The ads were meant to make fun of Guy and it wasn't easy for him and his family to listen to them. But the ads actually seemed to help, rather than hurt, Guy's chances of being elected. Most Alabamians identified with Hunt's country-boy roots and they didn't like having others make fun of those roots.

The closer it got to Election Day, the more people gathered around Guy. On November 4, 1986, over one million people voted in the Alabama governor's race – 696,203 of them marked their ballot for Harold Guy Hunt. It was more votes than any other Alabama governor had ever received.

On election night, Guy listened while the CBS Evening News called out his name as the next governor of Alabama. It was hard to believe that he had

**

won, and especially hard to believe that a Republican would actually be Alabama's top elected official. It was something that had not happened in Alabama for more than 100 years.

A happy and victorious Guy Hunt and wife, Helen.

Alice Yeager

A Republican Governor? Surely A Mistake!

NOVEMBER 5th, THE DAY AFTER Hunt's election, found many Alabamians scratching their heads and asking, "How in the world did a Republican get elected as governor in Alabama?"

No one enjoyed the confusion that clouded his election more than Guy Hunt himself. "I caused one publisher to have to rewrite an Alabama history book for fourth grade students. It was written just after Charles Graddick won the first primary and listed him as being elected governor in November, 1986 . . . I'll have to say I am not sorry they had to rewrite it."

A powerful Democratic state senator called Governor Hunt's election, "the beginning of the power of the Republican Party in Alabama." Then he added, "and the Democrats did it to themselves." Most Democrats weren't the least bit happy about having a Republican in the Governor's Mansion. They said that Alabamians would be sorry that Hunt had been elected, and predicted that after four years of his leadership, it would probably take another hundred years for a Republican to be elected again.

At first nobody took Governor Hunt seriously. They thought he would serve four years, go back to little Holly Pond, and be forgotten. But Guy Hunt was eager to prove them wrong, "Some expected me to be only a figurehead governor . . . to be but a blip on the political scene."

It didn't take long for people to start changing their minds. One newspaper article compared Hunt to

After the inauguration, Hunt still favored the same kinds of food he grew up with, but now his dining room table was in the Governor's Mansion in Montgomery.

Benjamin Meek Miller, the light bulb-toting governor who had been in office when Hunt was born. The writer of the article said that not since Miller's time in office had Alabama elected such an honest governor. Another reporter compared Hunt's story of rising from farmer to governor to that of Abraham Lincoln's story, "The moral of the story is that even someone who doesn't have $1 million can become governor of Alabama."

86

Governor Guy Hunt with members of the band Alabama and others in the Governor's Mansion.

Epilogue

Sometimes people change when they are given political power. Sometimes they start thinking that they are better than others. Not Guy Hunt. When it was time for the family to load up, leave Holly Pond, and head for Montgomery, Governor Hunt looked at his children and told them to remember something very important, "We're going to come back here just like we left here – don't let this go to your head."

During the final weeks of campaigning when people were beginning to predict that the Democrats were going to lose, Hunt told crowds that if elected, he would throw the biggest *whimdoozie* of all. No one knew what that meant, so Guy explained they would have catfish fries all over the state to celebrate – his word whimdoozie meant that something was a big deal, and Guy Hunt being elected governor would certainly be a whimdoozie.

Even though the election had taken place in November 1986, the new governor was not sworn into office until January 19, 1987. This was the day that he would officially become Alabama's 54th governor. Governor Hunt started his inaugural speech by thanking Alabamians for giving him such an honor. He promised to serve with honesty and integrity and to help our state become so great that people would always be proud to say "I'm from Alabama." He wanted all voters to come together – instead of fighting as Republicans and Democrats – he asked everyone to pull together, "We now are *one* Alabama . . ."

He talked of plans to make Alabama better and stronger as he mentioned *A New Day . . . A New Alabama*, and by ending his speech with, "As your governor, I say to you from the bottom of my heart that I have no ambition other than to serve you well with honesty and integrity. With your help, and with Divine guidance, I will make you the best governor Alabama has ever had." His first day of being governor continued with parties and parades, and the night was filled with Inaugural balls or dances.

It was after midnight before the new governor crawled into bed. He was bone tired – all 6 foot 2 inches of him – but it was the best feeling in the world. The next morning he woke up and warm memories of all that had taken place the day before drifted through his mind. His eyes twinkled with mischief as he leaned over and gently kissed Helen. "Have you ever been kissed by a governor?"

She paused a moment to think, and then answered, "No."

First Four Years in Office

Once in office, Governor Hunt started putting his ideas for a new Alabama into place. Even people who believed that Hunt had only made it to the governor's mansion because of the fighting among Democrats were impressed. They soon realized the governor's ideas were good ones, and legislators at the State Capitol were overheard saying, "Guy Hunt may talk slow, but he sure doesn't think slow."

Alabama's governor enjoying a game of horseshoes, and showing President Bush, far left, the pleasures of the game.

One of Governor Hunt's main concerns was that big businesses rarely considered our state when looking for a place to locate. He knew that bringing new businesses to Alabama would mean more money for our economy. Hunt, along with others who worked closely with him, came up with the slogan – *"Alabama is Open for Business."* They found a way to make sure their slogan was seen all over America. They placed a large billboard in New York City letting everyone know that Alabama wanted their business.

The governor's office also came up with another way to bring people to our state with a project called the *Alabama Reunion*. They asked families to plan get-togethers and invite friends and family members who lived away to come back for a visit. People were encouraged to celebrate Alabama's rich history and the governor challenged big cities and small communities to plan special homecomings. The Hunts planned a few gatherings themselves. Guy's classmates from Holly Pond High School came to the governor's mansion for their 37th class reunion. Thirty-five out of forty-three graduating members attended the reunion with their husbands and wives, and they came from as far away as Michigan.

Helen listened to her husband's plans and decided to help with one project herself. She took a particular interest in the *Adopt-A-Mile* program – this was an anti-litter campaign to get people involved with cleaning up state highways. The campaign fit right in with the *Alabama Reunion* project. The way Helen looked at it, when company comes to visit us, we clean up and make everything look nice. Since company would be coming home to Alabama, it was time to clean up our state – Helen wanted people to treat Alabama's highways as they would their own homes. The *Adopt-A-Mile* project printed signs with the names of people who had volunteered to pick up litter on highways near their homes or businesses. Helen and Guy chose a two-mile strip near their farm and each weekend

As Governor and First Lady, Guy and Helen found themselves as Alabama's lead ambassadors at many events, including this Nascar race.

when they returned home to Holly Pond, the two of them walked the roadside and removed any trash that had been dropped by litterbugs.

After a year in office, Governor Hunt's ideas were being noticed not just by Alabamians, but by people throughout the United States. *U.S. News and World Report* listed him as one of America's best governors after seeing his successful efforts to bring businesses to Alabama.

Even as governor, Guy still spent his weekends serving church members. He was the only preacher ever to be elected as an Alabama governor and he was also the only elected official in the United States who kept on preaching while serving as governor. He continued preaching at Mount Vernon and at another small church in the Holly Pond area, Gum Pond Primitive Baptist.

Every weekend the Hunts headed back to Cullman County. The closer they got to their hometown, the happier they were. Guy's easy-going smile stretched even bigger when reaching the edge of town and reading signs that welcomed visitors to Holly Pond. Sometimes he still found it hard to believe that their words could be true, but he loved seeing the markers that read, "Holly Pond, home of Governor Guy Hunt."

Alice Yeager

Second Term in Office

At the end of his four-year term, Guy wanted to keep serving as Alabama's governor, but the Democrats were more determined than ever to take back the governor's office.

Once again they tried making fun of Hunt's farming background during the campaign by calling him "Governor Gomer," comparing him to Gomer Pyle on the *Andy Griffith Show*. But Governor Hunt decided to outsmart them at their own game. When he saw a Democrat with a bumper sticker that said, *Gomer,*

Guy outsmarted his competition, recognizing the fondness that Alabamians had for George "Goober" Lindsey and Jim "Gomer" Nabors, fellow Alabamians who performed as country boys on the popular Andy Griffith television show.

Goober and Guy, he had thousands of the bumper stickers printed and gave them out to his supporters. He realized something that the Democrats had failed to think about . . . people loved the *Andy Griffith Show* and they loved Gomer and Goober. Millions of people still watched reruns because they enjoyed Mayberry's folksy, down-home characters. A slogan that was meant to make Governor Hunt look silly, actually ended up being a great campaign strategy.

The governor's race of 1990 was close, but when all votes were counted, Alabamians had re-elected Guy Hunt for another term as governor.

Governor Hunt was eager to make the next four years as successful as his first term in office. He continued many of the projects that were started during his first term. He also continued to encourage people to serve as Republicans, and he worked to make the party grow stronger by appointing fellow Republicans to state positions.

Many people had given campaign fund money to help Guy Hunt get elected. That money paid for Governor Hunt to talk to Alabamians on television, to travel around the state meeting voters, and to pay workers to help with the many things that have to be done when someone runs for governor.

When he was elected, people also contributed

money for the celebrations and parties that were held around the time Governor Hunt was to be sworn in. That money was called the "Inaugural Fund."

The campaign money and the inauguration money was supposed to be kept separate. Many people helped keep track of the money. Some mistakes were made. Some campaign money and some inauguration money got put in the same account, which legally was not supposed to happen.

When it was discovered, some people accused Governor Hunt of breaking ethics rules.

Questions were raised about how the money was being spent. Before it was over, Hunt was convicted of misusing the money. Hunt had to leave the governor's office, serve five years of probation, was ordered to spend 1,000 hours working in his community for no pay, plus pay $200,000 that he was accused of misusing.

Hunt always stood firm that he was not guilty. And on June 11, 1997, the Alabama Board of Pardons and Paroles agreed. They pardoned Hunt on grounds that he was innocent of misusing the money.

On the very afternoon that Hunt's probation was lifted, he dropped by the Republican headquarters and registered to run for governor again. But Alabamians chose not to send him back to Montgomery.

Two years later, voters were no kinder during Hunt's 2002 bid for the state senate . . . again, he lost.

During their last years together, the Hunts lived on the farm that they loved, tending to beehives, gardening and taking care of orchards filled with nectarines, pears, peaches, apples and plums.

Guy continued to preach until his death in 2009.

Alice Yeager

How Will Governor Hunt Be Remembered?

Time has a way of dulling our memories so that only the things that are talked of loudest or that are written about most will survive. One hundred years from now when the name Guy Hunt is mentioned, will someone ask, "Guy Hunt? Isn't he the governor that was removed from office?"

This was the very thing that the man from Holly Pond feared most. In a 1998 interview, he shared how he wanted to be remembered with a *New York Times* reporter. "The thing that would thrill me the most is if every fourth-grade student in this state who reads Alabama history someday will have the understanding that this is an honest governor who ran an honest administration and would not knowingly violate the letter or spirit of the law . . . That's what's important to me."

Certainly, history books will not ignore the fact that Hunt and his 1986 election made it possible for other Republicans to be elected to office in Alabama. When Republican Bob Riley was elected as governor in 2002, Hunt pointed out that Republicans had been elected to the governor's office 16 out of the last 20 years . . . and then he added, "it all began with my election in 1986."

Also remembered will be Hunt's successful efforts to make state government more efficient, his effort to get laws passed that would reduce the number of lawsuits (government leaders called it "tort reform"), and his success in reaching out to big business and bringing more industry to Alabama. He also will be remembered for working hard to bring more tourists to Alabama.

But perhaps, Guy Hunt will be remembered by his own description of himself during his second inaugural speech, "I do not possess great wealth . . . I do not flaunt great political power . . . I am a farmer and a farmer's son . . . a country preacher with a country family and country values . . . I am proud of what I am."

Harold Guy Hunt

June 17, 1933 Born in Holly Pond, Alabama.

Spring 1950 Graduated from high school at age sixteen.

February 25, 1951 Married childhood sweetheart Helen Chambers.

January 1953 Began speaking in the Primitive Baptist Church.

July 13, 1954 Entered military service; served with the 101st Airborne Division and the 1st Infantry.

October 1, 1954 Daughter Pamela born

December 30, 1956 Daughter Sherrie born

September 1958 Ordained as Primitive Baptist gospel minister.

May 9, 1959 Son Keith born

Guy Hunt: Governor Who Leveled The Field

1962 Unsuccessfully ran on the Republican ticket for State Senator.

February 23, 1963 Daughter Lynn born

1964 Elected Cullman County Probate Judge; youngest probate judge in Alabama; served six years and was re-elected in 1970.

1976 & 1980 Chaired Alabama's Republican delegation at the National Conventions.

1978 Ran for governor but was defeated by Fob James. Won every voting box in Cullman County.

1980 Appointed State Chairman of Ronald Reagan's Presidential Campaign.

May 1981 Appointed by President Ronald Reagan as State Executive Director of the Agricultural Stabilization and Conservation Service (ASCS) of the Department of Agriculture.

November 4, 1986 Elected first Republican Governor of Alabama in 112 years by defeating Lieutenant Governor Bill Baxley.

January 19, 1987 Inaugurated Alabama's 54th governor.

December 1987 *U.S. News and World Report* magazine identified Hunt as one of the eleven best governors in America.

November, 1990 Re-elected governor of Alabama by defeating Democratic nominee Paul Hubbert.

January 14, 1991 Inaugurated governor for a second term.

April 22, 1993 Removed from governor's office for violation of the ethics act.

June 11, 1997 Alabama Board of Pardons and Paroles pardoned Hunt on grounds of innocence, but most of the $200,000 that was to be paid back to a court fund was still owed; Hunt was still serving probation.

March 30, 1998 Hunt's probation was lifted after Alabamians raised money to pay off the balance owed to the court fund.

June 1998 Ran for governor, but failed to make the Republican runoff.

Fall 2002 Unsuccessfully ran for Alabama Senate.

November 22, 2004 Helen Hunt died from pulmonary fibrosis at age 70.

October 14, 2005 Married longtime family friend Anne Smith. Anne's husband had died of cancer just before Helen passed away. As friends, she and Guy were a great comfort to each other. Only three months after their wedding, Guy was diagnosed with lung cancer. Anne remained by Guy's side, taking care of him during a three-year battle with cancer.

March 2006 Hunt attended the grand opening for *Helen's House*, a group home for mentally retarded and developmentally disabled adults near Holly Pond. In 2010, Pamela Hunt and two other females along with their caregivers live at the time of this writing at *Helen's House*. Money to purchase the home was donated by the board that oversaw the court-ordered fund from Guy's trial since it ordered that the funds be used for charitable purposes. Former Governor Hunt told the crowd he felt sure that Helen was smiling down from Heaven – she had always worried about Pamela being taken care of when she and Guy were no longer living. Both Helen and Guy had always considered Pamela a blessing, and taking care of Alabama's special needs children was something that was near and dear to the former First Lady's heart.

May 2006 A new rest stop on I-65 near Cullman was named in honor of Guy Hunt by the Alabama Highway Department.

January 30, 2009 Guy Hunt died from lung cancer at age 75. More than 1,000 people attended his funeral at Snead State Community College in Boaz. He was buried beside Helen at Mount Vernon Church, in Cullman County's Fairview Community, where he had preached for 54 years.

About the Author

Alice Yeager lives with her husband Tim on Shoals Creek in Killen, Alabama. She loves history and has written about several other famous Alabamians through the *Alabama Roots Series*. Just recently, she has also been involved with the filming of several documentaries about historical landmarks in north Alabama.

Alice served as an elementary teacher, guidance counselor and curriculum specialist before leaving public schools to work with Alabama's voluntary preschool programs. She enjoys reading, boating, taking moonlight walks along the river, tending to stray animals and traveling all over this amazing state that she proudly calls home.